Troublemaker

MW01609070

Surviving

Hollywood and

Scientology

Summary and Analysis

By Summary Station

Copyright © 2015 by Summary Station

All rights reserved. This book or any portion thereof
may not be reproduced or used in any manner whatsoever
without the express written permission of the publisher
except for the use of brief quotations in a book review.

Printed in the United States of America

First Printing, 2015

Table of Contents

Chapter 1

When Leah was growing up she always wanted to be an entertainer. She began auditioning for plays when she was still a very young girl. When she was only nine years old she auditioned for the lead role in a play on Broadway called Annie, but she did not get the part. Leah grew up in the city of Brooklyn, New York with her older sister Nicole in the Bensonhurst neighborhood. Leah and her family would take vacations to the nearby Poconos. The family was very close until the parents divorced around 1980. Leah recalls that her father was sometimes mean to her and her sister because he would yell at them and call them idiots, but this man was also very loving and he would show that he cared from time to time.

After Leah's parents divorced, her mother began to see a new man who was a Scientologist. Leah's mother began attending the Church of Scientology and she quickly made it a priority in her life. After some time, Leah and her sister Nicole started to go to the Church of Scientology in Manhattan with their mother and her boyfriend. After a series of indoctrination courses, both Leah Nicole became recruited by the Sea Organization which is a specialized group of Scientologists within the Church of Scientology. The Sea Organization consists of around 4,000 of the top Scientologists in the world and it was created by the founder of Scientology L. Ron Hubbard. In 1967 Hubbard was in England when he was forced to move his church onto a series of boats because he was not granted a visa in the United Kingdom. The Church of Scientology reports that there are about 10 million practitioners of scientology in the world today. However, Leah believes that this is a highly inflated number and the actual number is probably closer to about 35,000 people.

Chapter 2

Leah moved to Clearwater, Florida with her sister, mother, and stepfather when she was still young. This was a big move and it was not the only new change in Leah's life because her mother had become pregnant. Leah and her sister had also made a very big commitment to the Church of Scientology upon moving to Florida. The girls each signed contracts which stated that they would remain in the Sea Organization of the Church of Scientology for 1 billion years. The reason the church made the girls sign a contract for so long is because they believe that they will be reincarnated multiple times and this will allow them to live multiple lives.

After an extensive process Leah was allowed to stay in the Sea organization, but her sister was denied entry due to her admission of taking drugs many years ago. Work was a very important part of life within the Church of Scientology. Both Leah and Nicole worked for the church 12 hours a day at the Estates Project Force. Leah describes the Estates Project Force as a type of boot camp where the children would wear uniforms. Everything seemed like it was going steady until Leah's mother Vicki gave birth to her new child. Shortly after this birth, Vicki learned that her new husband was leaving her for another woman and he would not be moving to Florida.

Chapter 3

Leah was educated by the Sea Organization of the Church of Scientology. The Church of Scientology believes that traditional education is not valuable in comparison to an education in scientology. They believe that a child who is educated in scientology has what would be equal to a doctorate degree in the traditional education system. The Sea Organization operated multiple hotels and many of the guests who stayed there were practicing members of the church. The Church of Scientology held many training and auditioning sessions at these hotels so they were frequently filled with people.

Leah was given a job at one of the hotels and her job was to collect the tickets that people would use to pay for their meals. All of the hotels guests dined in the restaurant, but members of the Sea Organization had to eat in a separate area. This meant that Leah was isolated from much of the general public during her early years with the Church of Scientology. Leah really wanted to eat in the normal restaurant with everybody else so she found a way to make counterfeit meal tickets. She used the tickets for herself in order to buy food in the restaurant.

Leah takes a moment to tell about some of the policies and procedures that are associated with the Church of Scientology. There are a few organizations that are responsible for making sure that all the rules are followed. The Commodores Messenger Organization consists of members of the church who are dedicated to delivering messages to L. Ron Hubbard. The ethics organization consists of members and these members have a Master at Arms who is in charge of making sure that all of the rules are followed. There is also a method for members of the church to report on each other for not following rules and this is done by filling out a knowledge report.

The Church of Scientology has a very structured system that makes sure to keep track of all of its members so that they do not break any of the rules. The rules of Scientology go into extensive detail and actions are described as either being on policy or off policy. If an action is off policy and a member of the church commits this action, they will be subject to discipline. Many of the children who grow up in the Church of Scientology do not know any other way of life because they are told that the education that they receive from the Church of Scientology will be much more valuable than any other education they could get.

Chapter 4

Leah's mother Vicki got in trouble with the Sea Organization and she was going to be disciplined for her actions. She decided to take Leah and her sister away from the church and they moved in with a friend in Los Angeles, California. This was the first time that Leah lived in Hollywood. Even though the family moved away from the church, they were still spending much of their time studying Scientology and they did not enroll in any public or private schools. Since Leah and her sister dropped out of the Sea Organization they were subject to monetary debt. This was part of their contract and they felt obligated to pay off their debts to the Church of Scientology. Leah made an agreement with the church that she would be allowed to take Scientology courses for free as long as she remained a member. As soon as she decided to leave the church, all of the classes she had taken were no longer free and she was obligated to pay for the previous classes she had taken with the church.

One night, Leah decided to go out drinking with some of her friends and she was so hung over the next day that she was not able to make it to Scientology class. One of the church's policies is to make sure that all students are "on course" after 24 hours has passed since alcohol was drank. Leah's mother could not stand to see her go unpunished for disobeying the churches rules so she wrote up a knowledge report describing Leah's drinking. One of the Masters at Arms investigated the knowledge report that Leah's mother wrote and he decided to question Leah about her drinking. At first Leah did not want to tell her friends, but after some interrogation she decided to tell the Master at Arms who the other church members were that she went drinking with. Leah was led to believe that she would help her friends by informing the Master at Arms about their inability to follow the rules.

There are other religions that are known for keeping a close watch on their members, but this is mainly done during church functions. The Church of Scientology is unique because they keep a watch on their members at all times. This means that members of the church have very little privacy. Members of the Church of Scientology are instructed to trust each other and they are even supposed to hire other Scientologists for employment positions even when they are not qualified. Scientologists are always instructed to tell the truth no matter what the consequences or how guilty they feel about what might have taken place. The Church of Scientology instructs its members that the most noble and honorable action they can take is to tell the truth at all times.

Chapter 5

When Leah and her family first moved to Hollywood California they faced many financial burdens. The family did not even have enough money to buy furniture for their new home. The little money that they did have went towards paying for more Scientology literature to study and courses to attend. Leah even began working for an insurance company to make extra money for the family. Leah's mother Vicki got married once again to a new man named George. George moved into the house with Vicki's family and one of Vicki's friends named Sherri was still living there. Sherry was a member of the Sea Organization with the Church of Scientology and she also had connections in Hollywood because she was dating the brother of the actress named Juliet Lewis. Leah took this opportunity to have Sherry arrange auditions. Leah still desperately wanted to be an actress and she was ready to apply herself at the auditions. Even though Leah did not have much real acting experience and she was frequently rejected at acting auditions, she continued to work towards her goal of becoming an actress.

Leah was not only motivated to become an actress because it was her childhood dream, she also wanted to be an actress because she knew that it paid good money. Leah felt that if she were to become an actress it would raise her status within the Church of Scientology. She wanted to prove to the church that she was a responsible and respectable member. This would also allow Leah to advance up a few levels within the church organization and that was very motivating to her. There are many celebrities in the Church of Scientology and the celebrities are considered to be Opinion Leaders. The church places a high ranking on an Opinion Leader because they have trust in their ability to persuade others.

Leah felt that if she were to fail at getting an acting role she would be considered a failure by the Church of

Scientology. She believed that the information that was provided to her by the Church of Scientology should be enough for her to get an acting job if she is able to apply it in the correct manner. The church teaches all of its members that if they are successful in their careers they will have a greater impact on the church. Scientology also teaches its members that they are able beings who are capable of great achievements and that most others are just average and this makes them incapable of achievement.

Chapter 6

Leah was invited to audition for a new television series called living dolls. She prepared for this audition by having another Scientologist bombard her with questions about different Scientology courses. A group of fellow church members was gathered together to serve as an audience so that Leah would feel as though she were on an actual stage. She did so well at the addition that she won the part. Leah was so happy for this achievement and she felt that she owed it all to the Church of Scientology. After being awarded the role, Leah was invited to attend filming for a show called Who's the Boss. She spent a few weeks behind the scenes of this show because the show that she was going to be working on was a spinoff of Who's the Boss.

Leah quickly began to find that she was under a great deal of pressure due to all of the new responsibilities that came with acting on a television show. At times the stress would get to Leah, but the people at her church instructed her to keep on working. Now that Leah had a steady acting career she wanted to move her entire family to Burbank California so they would be closer to the production studio. Her older sister Nicole decided that she wanted to move away from the family and start her own life and this included dropping out of the Church of Scientology.

Chapter 7

Many of the early acting jobs that Leah had in Hollywood did not work out in the long run. One of the shows she was working on was canceled after only seven episodes. A few of the other shows she worked on never even broadcasted on television. She did act in a series of guest performances that did air on national television before she became famous. Leah was going out and acting for many additions and this made it very difficult for her to attend all of the church functions she was required to be at. The Church of Scientology did not show any leniency towards Leah and they required her to spend her required time every day just like everyone else.

Now that Leah was considered to be a professional actress she was allowed to attend the Celebrity Center at the Church of Scientology. This was an exclusive center for Hollywood actors and actresses like Kristie Alley, Tom Cruise, and John Travolta. Leah was somewhat disappointed that she did not encounter any of the celebrities that she knew of when she was at the celebrity center.

When L. Ron Hubbard created Scientology he intended for the practitioners to study the accompanying information until they knew it exactly perfect. Leah did not feel like she had an adequate amount of time to study the material to the extent that she needed to. It seemed to her like all of the other Scientology practitioners were given as much time as they needed. Leah had seen testing sessions that had taken over 20 hours to complete. This got her thinking about all the work that she had done and the expectations that she had in regards to what her status would be like in the Church of Scientology. She did not feel as though the progress she made was showing any real benefits.

Leah realized that she had to be careful about any thoughts she was having in regards to the church not meeting her expectations.　Members of the Church of Scientology are not allowed to think critically and it is a very serious offense to think critically about the Church of Scientology.　Scientology views any critical thought as being a sign that some kind of overt act has been taken. Scientologists believe that critical thinking is wrong because when a person thinks critical of someone else they are reflecting their own faults on another person.

Chapter 8

Leah does not prefer to date men who are also members of the Church of Scientology. This has been a preference of hers since she was younger and even during a seven year period of her life when she was promiscuous starting at the age of 18. Leah dated many men during her promiscuous time but one of the men that made a big impact on her was Angelo Pagan. Pagan and Leah became very close but Angelo was already married. Angelo did not tell Leah that he was married when he first met her, but he did tell her that he had a problem with cheating in relationships. Leah thought that the Church of Scientology would be able to help Angelo with his cheating problem so she helped him to enroll in a course there. At the time Leah had already completed many Scientology courses but she still cheated in her relationships too. Angelo had a wife and family which consisted of three children and neither he nor Leah wanted to break up the family. To make matters worse, Leah's mother did not condone the relationship because of Angelo's previous marriage.

It was only a matter of time before Leah felt that she needed to tell the Church of Scientology about her affair with Angelo. Having an affair with a married person went against the rules of the Church of Scientology so she knew that it was time to fess up and receive her punishment. The Church of Scientology decided to punish Leah by making her pay for Angelo and his wife to receive marriage counseling. Of course this marriage counseling would be offered by the Church of Scientology.

Angelo and his wife agreed when Leah asked them to attend the counseling services at the Church of Scientology. After all of the counseling was completed, Angelo and his wife came to a conclusion that they would remain married, but Angelo could still have girlfriends on the side. The only condition was that Angelo still had to come back to his family home every night. Apparently this arrangement did not work because shortly after the marriage counseling Angelo reported to Leah that he was going to leave his wife.

Chapter 9

Leah received an acting role on a new sitcom called Fired Up, but like many of the other acting positions she had in her early career, this too was canceled early. Fired Up was only broadcasted for one and a half seasons before it was dropped. When Leah found out that the show was canceled it was very difficult for her to accept. She felt as though the failure of the show was a reflection of a failure on her part. She was doubting her ability to be an actress and she felt as though she let down the Church of Scientology. As a result of this show's cancellation, Leah decided that it would be best for her to dedicate more of her time to Scientology.

Many people in the entertainment industry still believed that Leah was a good actress so they kept her in mind for future projects. Leah had left acting behind to focus on scientology when she was contacted about an acting role in a new show called The King of Queens. At first Leah did not want to even audition for the role because she doubted her acting ability. Kevin James and less Moonves were already working with the new show and they felt that Leah would be a perfect fit so they went out of their way and convinced her to audition. The addition very well for the part and it was offered to her so she accepted it.

The King of Queens became one of America's most popular television shows and this show is mainly responsible for introducing many people all over the world to Leah. Everyone else on the show knew from the start that Leah was a member of the Church of Scientology and she took this role very seriously. No one had a problem with this and everyone did their best to keep this information private. Everything went well for the first five years of the shows broadcasting, but something happened in between the fifth and sixth seasons of the show that caused alarm to Leah. There was news that the show would be moving to a different timeslot in the network schedule. Leah began to question if this was because of something that she might have done wrong and she began to become anxious. The anxiety began to get worse and Leah remembers that she started to hear a voice in her mind that spoke of bad things to come in the future. Leah took her troubles to the Church of Scientology and they enrolled her in courses to help her get this negative voice out of her head.

Chapter 10

Everything was going well in Leah's career and she began to advance in the Church of Scientology as well. A review was conducted where Leah was to talk with the Church of Scientology about everything she had done since she began attending the church. This was done as a sort of test to determine whether or not Leah was ready to advance to the next level of Scientology. After Leah completed this review, one of the members of the church suggested that she should get married because that would increase her chance of progressing to the next level. Leah did not waste much time before getting married and she had her first daughter whom she named Sophia.

Leah was not adjusting well to becoming a mother. She found that she was stretching herself thin and not getting enough sleep. The new crying baby at home was the main reason that she was missing out on sleep and she went to the Church of Scientology for answers on how to get the baby to stop crying so much. Leah was told by the church that the baby was crying because either Leah was not applying her Scientology teachings correctly or there was something wrong with the home environment.

Leah was advised by the Church of Scientology that she should not take drugs to assist with childbirth. The church is against using any kind of drugs when a woman is giving birth because they believe it will have a negative influence on the baby which will cause it to be wrongly impacted by sounds that are made during the birth. In fact, the Church of Scientology advises the members of the church that it is best if there is no noise taking place in a room when a child is being born.

Chapter 11

The Church of Scientology provided Leah with materials and information to help her raise her child. She decided that she did not want to raise her child with the help of any of the church's information so she did it on her own. She realized that she could use some help so she hired a nanny and this nanny was not a member of the Church of Scientology. The Church of Scientology prefers that mothers only hire nannies who are also involved with the church. Leah spent every free opportunity she had watching her child play around. However, many times she was too tired to play with her child. This was because her role on The King of Queens required her to spend most of her time working on the show. In addition to the demands at work, the Church of Scientology had moved her up to the next level which was known as Operating

Thetan. Any day that Leah had off from her job as an actress was spent at the Church of Scientology.

During the time that Leah was studying for her new role with the church she was relocated to the same church in Clearwater, Florida that she used to attend when she was with the Sea Organization. She had forgotten all about the times when she used to make counterfeit meal tickets to get free food when she was a child and returning to Clearwater brought back these memories. Leah felt that the right thing to do was to tell the Church of Scientology about the transgressions she made when she was a child. The church decided that her punishment should be a $40,000 cash donation to the church to make up for the food that she ate. This was the beginning of Leah's break up with the Church of Scientology. Leah was still in contact with former members of the church and she used her role in the church to speak for the people who were no longer members. This speaking out was something that the Church of Scientology did not like and it created tension between Leah and the church.

Chapter 12

Due to Leah's celebrity status she was advised by the church to donate money to charitable organizations. However these charitable organizations must be supported by the church. In addition to donating money, Leah was advised that she should donate her time to making public appearances in the name of promoting the Church of Scientology. Leah agreed with the church and she began to donate money to charitable organizations.

One of the organizations that Leah donated money to is called The International Association of Scientologists and Leah's involvement with this organization was responsible for her meeting other famous celebrities. One of the celebrities that Leah began associating with was Tom Cruise and in the Church of Scientology he is known as Mr. Cruise. The Church of Scientology provides Mr. Cruz with an entourage that mainly consists of Sea Organization members whose main purpose is to protect him. They are assigned to specifically protect Mr. Cruz from anyone who might happen to offend him.

Leah learned that Tom Cruise is one of the highest ranking members of the Church of Scientology and the church is supportive of everything he says and does. When Tom Cruise married actress Katie Holmes they had a wedding that was put together by the Church of Scientology. This was a major wedding that would reflect the Church of Scientology so the church made sure to involve most of its top players for the planning of the event.

Chapter 13

This chapter focuses on Tom Cruise and Katie Holme's wedding. This event took place in Rome, Italy and it was covered by all of the major media networks across the globe. The Church of Scientology was very excited about its opportunity to create good public relations and show the world that the church had a big impact on the entertainment business in Hollywood. Miscavige is one of the highest-ranking officials with the Church of Scientology and he personally attended this wedding. Many people thought that he would attend this wedding with his wife, but he showed up with his female assistant instead.

Leah thought it was quite strange that Miscavige's wife Shelley was not at the wedding. She began asking other people who were in attendance at the wedding if they knew anything about why Shelley was not there. Leah was surprised to find that people were being very uncooperative when it came to answering questions regarding Shelley and they told her that they did not want to be involved with that kind of conversation. Some of the members of the church even told Leah that she did not have a high enough ranking to be inquiring about Shelley. Leah and Shelley were friends at the time so this was something that was upsetting to Leah. This incident made a big impact on Leah so she decided to record everything that happened to her at the wedding. She wrote out this information onto a knowledge report and delivered it to the proper location at the Church of Scientology.

Leah noticed many of the rules that were set by the Church of Scientology were broken by Tom Cruise and no one seemed to care. She felt that it was her duty as a scientologist to report what she had seen and she did not feel that she would be punished for doing so. The Church of Scientology states that they view all of their practitioners as equal, but Leah did not see this happening at Tom and Katie's wedding.

Chapter 14

As soon as Leah got back to America she was instructed to go to a location known as Flag. This was the Church of Scientology location in Clearwater, Florida where Leah had spent many of her previous years. She was told that this visit was to prepare for her new level advancement with the church. This was simply a trick to get Leah to appear and think that nothing was wrong. When she arrived at the church in Florida, she discovered that the real reason she was called down there was to talk about the knowledge reports she had written in addition to reports that were written about her when she was at the wedding in Italy.

Many knowledge reports had been filed at the wedding and they accused Leah of being drunk and disruptive. One of these reports was even written by Katie Holmes.

The Church of Scientology took these reports very seriously and they questioned Leah for about 12 hours each day over the course of a few weeks. After the interrogation Leah decided to withdraw the reports she had filed and pretend that everything went well at the wedding. Leah was also enrolled in a reprogramming course that would last several weeks. After Leah completed the reprogramming course she was invited to appear in a documentary supporting the Church of Scientology and this documentary was produced by BBC. After all of the dust had settled Leah decided to return to Hollywood, California.

Chapter 15

The King of Queens was on television for 207 episodes before being canceled. This marked a big transition in Leah's life. She still enjoyed acting and wanted to have a part in a new television show. A CBS show called The talk is a daytime talk show with all women hosts and Leah was invited to become one of the hosts for a year. This proved to be a very difficult show for Leah because she did not get along very well with some of the other hosts. The six different women hosts tended to have frequent conflicts with each other and Leah was involved with some of these conflicts. Many of these conflicts were over the guests who were picked to appear on the show and the topics that were discussed. Due to the conflict that Leah had with some of the other hosts, the producers of the show decided not to invite her back for a second year.

The Church of Scientology taught Leah that not getting invited back for another year as a host on The View was due to something that she did wrong. She went to the Church of Scientology and began to study more about scientology to get some insight on what she did wrong. Leah came to the conclusion that there was some good and bad from the situation and the good was that she was able to learn about who her actual friends are. This situation also enlightened Leah about the value of friendship and she began to become more grateful for her friends and family. Leah believes that it is difficult to find good friends in life and this is even more difficult in a place like Hollywood, California.

Chapter 16

Tom Cruise and Katie Holmes had a daughter together after their marriage and they named her Suri. As their daughter began to grow up, Katie decided that she did not want her exposed to the Church of Scientology. Tom Cruise had a problem with this and this was one of the reasons behind their decision to get a divorce. After the divorce, the Church of Scientology decided to label Katie Holmes as a suppressive person. This had a big effect on Leah because this meant that the knowledge reports Katie had filed on Leah at the wedding would be no longer considered valid by the church. When a member of the Church of Scientology is labeled as a suppressive person any reports that they have filed will become no longer supported by the church. When Leah found out about this she asked the church about getting back the money she spent on the reprogramming courses which came as a result of the knowledge reports that Katie had filed.

Leah met with her friend Shelley's husband David Miscavige about being re-compensated for everything that happened as a result of the wedding. After Leah met up with David she was informed by other members of the church that there was more rule breaking going on than she was previously aware of. This really got Leah thinking about Tom Cruise and his representation of the church. The Church of Scientology remained on the side of Tom Cruise and this caused a great deal of tension between Leah and the church. This is not something that Leah could not get over so she decided to leave the church. This is a huge decision because she no longer communicates with anyone representing the Church of Scientology.

Chapter 17

Right around the time that Leah broke her ties with the Church of Scientology she filed a missing person's report for Shelley Miscavige. The LAPD received the report and they began investigating the matter, but after they contacted the Church of Scientology about the whereabouts of Shelley they were directed to the church's lawyers. These lawyers told the LAPD that Shelley was in good health and she did not want people to know about her whereabouts. Leah believed that the Church of Scientology made an example of the situation in order to decimate Leah's character. This event also caused the Church of Scientology to label Leah as a suppressive person. Leah believes that the Church of Scientology did not make her a better person but it did make her a better Scientologist.

Chapter 18

Looking back on the events, Leah believes that Scientology did not have as big of an impact on her life as she used to believe. Leah felt that the church attempted to destroy her career after she became a suppressive person and this helped her to realize that the church never had her best interests in mind. Leah was with the Church of Scientology for over 30 years before she left and this departure caused some emotional instability mainly from cutting ties with friends and associates.

When Leah left the church, she was afraid that something horrible is going to go wrong in her life. This caused a great deal of stress and anxiety. After spending some time in the real world Leah began to meet many successful and happy people who did not rely on the Church of Scientology. This gave her confidence to believe that she did not really need the church or its teachings. She began to see the church as a type of cult. The church has one leader who can never be questioned and if any one of the followers breaks one of the many rules they will be strictly punished.

Today, Leah has rebuilt her group of friends so that she is no longer affected by the events of the past. The Church of Scientology was asked about their attempts to ruin Leah's acting career and they responded by saying that they did not care about what happened to her after she left the church and this was just an example of her self-absorbed personality. Leah believes that this is another example of what the Church of Scientology will do to anyone who speaks out against them.

Analysis

In "Troublemaker: Surviving Hollywood and Scientology" Leah Remini tells her readers about a list she made which includes the things in her life that she is not proud of. The items on this list include cheating, lying, and not being considerate of others. She even goes on to include her family members and the problems they had with each other.

Remini has a good reason for including this list of things she is not proud of in the beginning of her book. She is worried that the Church of Scientology might make these faults known to the world in an attempt to defame her character. Because of this, Remini wanted to be the first one to tell her story to the world. Some of the things that she lists as being problems in her past are still plaguing her in the present moment. Remini has been a member of the Church of Scientology for about 30 years and out of all this time the Church of Scientology was unable to teach her how to eliminate her negative faults.

The concept and central ideologies of the Church of Scientology have been quite alluring to Remini and other followers. The Church of Scientology advertises itself as a center for learning a scientific process that people can use to eliminate life's limitations with the intention of reaching life's full potential. The requirements for followers of the Church of Scientology are very demanding. A practitioner of Scientology must dedicate at least 2 1/2 hours each day to Scientology matters. Many people believe that the Church of Scientology creates division among its followers because it teaches them that they are against the rest of the world. The Church of Scientology is also very demanding financially and Remini can attest to this as she claims to have donated over $5 million during her time as a member of the church.

The church is also somewhat selective as it labels its members. If the Church of Scientology feels that one of its members is critical in any way of the church it will label that member as a suppressive person. Once a member is labeled as a suppressive person they will be shunned by other Scientology members and discredited by the church. Even though Remini has dedicated many hours of her life and many dollars of her salary to the Church of Scientology, she has still been labeled as a suppressive person.

Thanks for Reading

Hello, this message is from the readers and writers at Summary Station. We hope that you enjoyed this summary/analysis and that it has helped your life in some way. It is our intention to create information that our readers will find useful and valuable.

We fell grateful for the opportunity to have people read our books and we are even more grateful when our readers leave a review. Please leave a review that lets us know what you liked about this book so that we can work on improving future books.

About Summary Station

Many great books are released every year and most avid readers know that they may never have time to read all of the books on their list. In today's world, many people do not get as much time to read as they would like, so it is important to use any reading time wisely. The problem with this is that it can be very difficult to know if a book is worth reading until you have already invested some time into reading it.

This is one of the many reasons that Summary Station was created. The staff at Summary Station wants to provide readers with a way to get a good idea of a book before they invest their time and money into reading it. We make sure to provide you with as much information about a book as we possibly can.

With Summary Station you can be assured that you will not only get a quality summary of a featured book, but you will also receive valuable information and analysis. The themes and characters are discussed in each summary as well as a brief review of the featured book. Even if you know you are going to definitely read a book, it will give you a big advantage in understanding the book if you explore one of our excellent summaries first.

31560323R00032

Made in the USA
San Bernardino, CA
13 March 2016